Beginning GOLF

Golf instructor Peter Krause and the following athletes were photographed for this book:
Nick Berg,
Gabe Hilmoe,
Matt Hilmoe,
Sarah Hilmoe,
Angie Rizzo,
Reed Tauer,
Jenny Tollette.

Beginning
GOLF

Julie Jensen

Adapted from
Peter Krause's *Fundamental Golf*

Photographs by Andy King

Lerner Publications Company ● Minneapolis

Library of Congress Cataloging-in-Publication Data

Jensen, Julie, 1957-
    Beginning Golf / by Julie Jensen ; adapted from Peter Krause's Fundamental Golf ; photographs by Andy King.
        p.   cm. — (Beginning Sports)
    Includes bibliographical references (p.) and index.
    ISBN 0-8225-3504-1
    1. Golf—Juvenile literature. [1. Golf.] I. King, Andy, ill. II. Krause, Peter, 1954- Fundamental golf. III. Title. IV. Series.
GV965.J46   1995
796.352—dc20

                                                94-37101
                                                    CIP
                                                    AC

Manufactured in the United States of America

1 2 3 4 5 6 - I/HP - 00 99 98 97 96 95

Photo Acknowledgments
Photographs are reproduced with the permission of: pp. 7, 9 (top), The Saint Andrew's Golf Club; p. 8, Trustees of the British Museum; p. 9 (bottom), USGA; p. 10, Rick Dole/Golden Bear International; p. 11, Dee Darden; p. 14, Nancy Smedstad/IPS, Courtesy of Tim Nelson; p. 19, Edvins Erkmanis.

All diagrams by Laura Westlund.

Contents

Chapter 1

HOW THIS GAME GOT STARTED

Games help to make our lives more fun. But more than one person is needed to play most games. There is one game that you can play alone or with other people. That game is golf.

Golf is played outdoors. Golfers use long, slender clubs to hit a little ball across the grass **course** into a small hole called the **cup**. Hitting the golf ball doesn't take a lot of strength. But you do have to think and plan your shots.

This photograph was taken in 1888. It is one of the first photographs of golf being played in the United States.

7

Paul Sandby painted this watercolor picture of golfers in 1746.

Thousands of years ago, Roman shepherds played a game by hitting stones with curved sticks. Games similar to golf were also played in Holland and Chile long ago. In fact, games like golf were probably played all over the world.

People in Scotland certainly played golf. Scottish golfers played alongside the ocean on sandy areas of land called "links." The term, **links,** is still used to describe a golf course. In 1744 a group of golfers in Edinburgh, Scotland, made up the first written rules of the game.

Golf was also popular with the people of Great Britain. Wherever the British began a colony, they took their game of golf with them. They brought golf to the thirteen colonies that would become the United States.

In 1888 John Reid, an American from Scotland, asked a friend in Scotland to send him a set of golf clubs. Back then, golf clubs had to be made by hand. Tom Morris Sr., Reid's friend, was well known for the clubs he made. He sent a set of clubs to Reid. Reid convinced others to try Morris's clubs. Morris was soon sending clubs to the United States as fast as he could make them.

Reid and his friends built the

first golf course in the United States, in Yonkers, New York. The course was in a pasture. But their course wasn't the only one for long. Golf was becoming popular all over the United States.

By 1894 golfers wanted to organize and govern the fast-growing sport. They formed the United States Golf Association (USGA), which sets the official rules for golf competition.

John Reid, left, helped introduce Americans to the game of golf in the late 1800s.

Theodore Havemeyer (in the straw hat) was the first president of the U. S. Golf Association.

Jack Nicklaus

When Jack Nicklaus was 10 years old, he began playing golf with his dad. When Jack was 13, he won the Ohio State Junior Championship. Eight years later, Jack joined the Professional Golfers Association tour. In his pro career, Jack has won 20 major tournaments and 50 other tournaments. That's more than any other professional golfer. Jack, whose nickname is the "Golden Bear," now plays on the Senior tour.

Golf continued to grow in the United States. In 1916 the top golfers of New York formed a national organization—the Professional Golfers Association of America (PGA). They wanted to tell more people about the game. They also wanted to make sure that people who said they were golf professionals really were.

As of January 1994, there were more than 25 million golfers in the United States. These golfers play on more than 14,000 golf courses in the United States. More than 23,000 golf professionals help golfers play better.

Some pro golfers play for cash prizes on professional tours. The male pros play on the PGA tour. Female pros compete on the Ladies' Professional Golf Association (LPGA) tour, which began in 1948.

Nancy Lopez

Nancy Lopez's dad took her golfing when she was eight years old. Nancy won her first tournament the next year when she was nine. She hasn't stopped winning since.

The high school in Roswell, New Mexico, where Nancy grew up, didn't have a girls' golf team. Nancy played on the boys' team and led Roswell High School to two state championships. After she graduated from high school, Nancy went to Tulsa University.

Nancy joined the Ladies' Professional Golf Association (LPGA) tour in 1977 when she was 21 years old. She won 9 tournaments in 1978.

Now, after winning 47 events in 16 years, Nancy is still playing on the LPGA Tour. She is also one of 13 women in the LPGA Hall of Fame.

Golfers who aren't pros still can compete against other golfers. Many high schools and colleges have teams, and most public courses have recreational leagues.

But many people play golf just to relax or enjoy the fresh air. They like to improve their skills and learn new ones.

Many golfers like the game because no one is trying to tackle you, block your shot, or make you miss a pitch. It is up to you to decide how you want to hit the ball. Then you must carry out that decision. Doing that can be a challenge.

Chapter 2

BASICS

To play golf, you need clubs. Golf clubs are expensive. Borrow clubs from a friend while you are getting started.

Nancy Lopez is a professional golfer who has won more than 40 tournaments. She learned to play when she was a kid by using one of her mother's clubs.

If you can't borrow clubs, you can rent them at most golf courses. Ask the pro for some clubs that fit your size and skill level. Once you know what kind of clubs you like—and you have saved enough money—the pro can help you decide which clubs to buy.

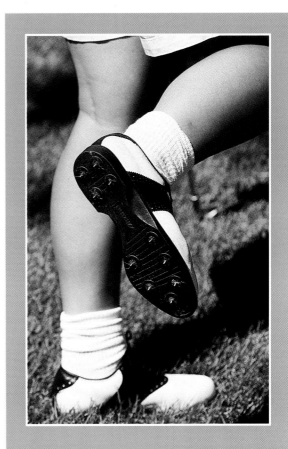

Golf Shoes

Golf shoes have short steel spikes that dig into the ground. You can wear gym shoes to play golf, but you may slip.

Golf Balls

A golf ball weighs about 1½ ounces and is about 1½ inches in diameter. There are three kinds of balls: solid piece, two piece, or three piece.
A solid-piece ball is molded out of a hard, synthetic material. This type of ball is good for beginning golfers.

A two-piece ball is a rubber ball surrounded by a Surlyn® cover. Surlyn is a hard plastic that is made by DuPont Company.

A three-piece ball is a small rubber ball that has rubber bands wrapped very tightly around it. The outer cover is a rubber material called balata. Balata is the dried sap from a West Indian tree, or the synthetic version of this sap. Professionals and very good golfers use balata balls. A balata ball will travel farther than the other balls,

but it is more likely to get damaged.
All golf balls have dimples stamped into their outer cover. The dimples help control the flight of the ball by affecting the way air flows around it. The size and pattern of the dimples vary from ball to ball. The more dimples on a ball, the lower and straighter its flight will be.

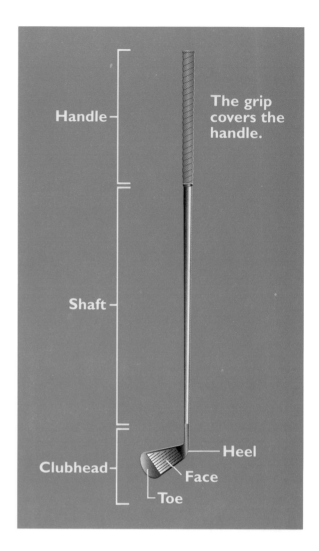

A set of clubs usually has 3 **woods**, 10 **irons**, and a **putter**, but a golfer can choose what combination of clubs to use. Each club has a handle, a shaft, and a clubhead. You hold the club by the grip on the handle. The shaft connects the handle and clubhead. You hit the ball with the clubhead.

Once, wood was the easiest material for people to find and make into a club. Now, most clubs—even woods—are made of steel. But woods, even when they're made of steel, are still called "woods."

When you first hit the ball, you want it to go far and straight. Woods are made to help you do this. Woods have longer shafts and bigger club-heads than the other clubs. The clubheads on woods are shaped like half-moons.

When you want the ball to go high into the air and not too far, you use an iron. The shafts of irons are shorter than woods. An iron's clubhead looks like an open hand tilted back toward the ground.

Irons have narrow channels running across the face of the clubhead. These grooves make the ball spin backward. This back spin makes the ball stop when it lands on the grass.

Once you are near the hole, you hit the ball with a putter to roll it into the cup.

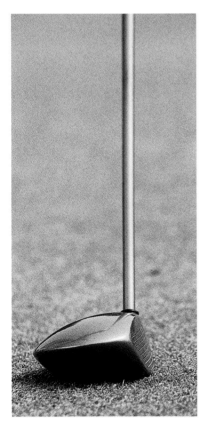

Wood

Iron

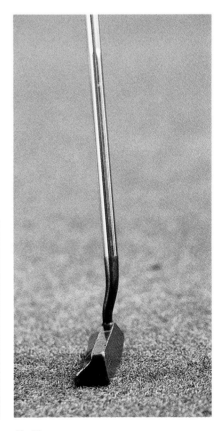

Putter

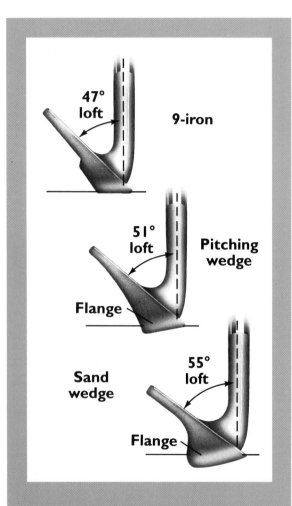

47°
loft

9-iron

51°
loft

Pitching
wedge

Flange

Sand
wedge

55°
loft

Flange

Pitching and Sand Wedges

A golfer uses a pitching wedge to lob the ball high into the air over trees, sand, water, and mounds.

A golfer uses a sand wedge to hit a ball out of the sand. A sand wedge has a wide, flat bottom, called a flange. This slides through the sand and under the ball. Wedges have the most loft of any clubs.

Hold an iron or wood with the clubhead touching the ground. See how the top of the clubhead tilts away from the bottom of the clubhead? This tilt is called **loft**. The more loft in a club, the higher the ball will go.

Numbers are stamped on the bottom of the clubs. Woods are numbered from 1 to 5. Irons are numbered from 1 to 10. Putters are not numbered.

High-numbered clubs hit the ball high into the air but not very far. Low-numbered clubs hit the ball far but not high. For example, a 9-iron has a lot of loft. A ball hit with a 9-iron will go higher into the air than a ball hit with a 4-iron. A 4-iron is a longer club with less loft. A 4-iron will make the ball go farther than a 9-iron will.

Each club's clubhead has a **toe**, a **face**, and a **heel**. When a golf ball is hit with the center of the face, it will spin backward as it travels toward the target. This spin helps the ball to go straight toward the target.

If the ball is hit with the toe of the clubhead behind the heel, the ball will spin from left to right. The ball's flight will curve to the right of a right-handed golfer (to the left of a left-handed golfer). This is called a **slice**.

If the toe of the club is in front of the heel when it hits the ball, the ball will spin from right to left. The ball's flight will curve to the left of a right-handed golfer for a **hook**. The ball will go to the right of a left-hander.

Chapter 3

THE SWING

In baseball and tennis, a player hits a moving ball. In golf, the ball stays still on the ground until it's hit. This should make golf easier, but that's the tricky part of this game. First, you have to learn how to swing the club. Then, you must swing it that way every time.

Once you have learned how to swing correctly, you can hit the ball with any club—except the putter—using this swing. The club you use determines how far the ball will travel.

A Tiger with His Woods

Eldrick (Tiger) Woods won the U.S. Junior Amateur Golf Tournament in 1991. He was just 15 years old, and he was the first black champion. In 1994, when Tiger was 18, he won the U.S. Amateur. He was the youngest winner in tournament history.

Home on the Range

Practice ranges give golfers a place to practice their shots. Most public courses have practice ranges. There are also practice ranges that are separate from courses. These often have practice putting greens too.

At the range, you rent a bucket of balls. Then you find an open space. All the golfers at the range hit in the same direction. Often, the practice range has targets that golfers can use to improve their aim. The targets may be flags or other structures.

No two people are exactly alike, so no two golf **swings** are alike either. A golfer's height, arm length, and athletic ability affect his or her swing.

Three elements, however, go into every swing: the **grip,** the **set-up,** and a mental image of the correct swing.

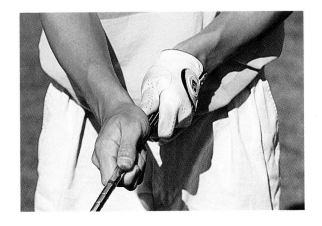

The Grip

First Nick must hold the club. A golfer's method for holding a club is called a grip.

Nick is right-handed. He places the fingers of his right hand on the club where the handle and shaft meet. Then, Nick lifts the club up to his waist with the toe of the club pointing to the sky.

Nick brings up his left hand and "shakes hands" with the end of the handle. He slides his right hand up the handle toward the left hand. Nick's right pinky covers his left forefinger. The rest of his hand is over his left thumb. If Nick were left-handed, he would do the same thing but with the opposite hands.

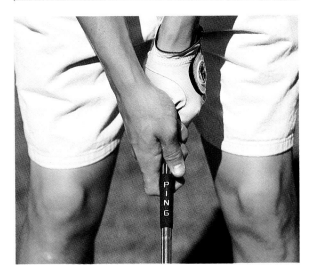

The Set-Up

To aim the club correctly, Nick first finds a target. Next, he thinks of a railroad track going to his target. He imagines that his ball is on the outside rail. He pretends that he is standing on the inside rail. His feet, knees, hips, and shoulders are all the same distance from the outside rail.

With his club in front of his waist, Nick bends from his hips. His knees are bent, and his weight is on the balls of his feet. In the photograph, you can see a yellow pole in the ground. Nick and his coach use the pole to make sure Nick's club and body are in the correct position for his swing.

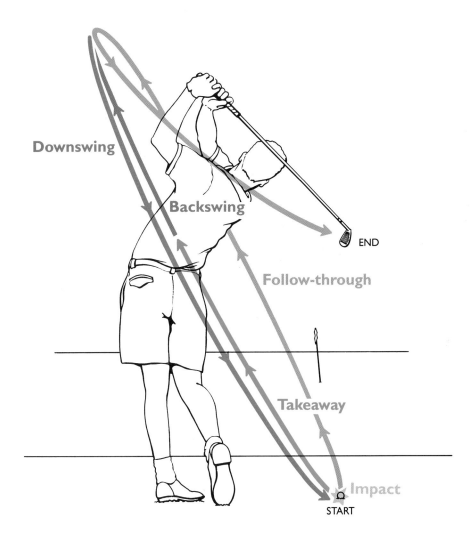

The Mental Image

Now Nick imagines a swing that is a mix of two motions. Because Nick is standing next to the ball, he must swing his club in a semi-circular motion. Since the ball is on the ground, Nick has to swing the club in an up-and-down motion.

When Nick correctly blends the two motions, he hits the ball with the club face pointing at the target. If Nick's swing is too circular or too up-and-down, the club face will be out of position when he hits the ball.

The Swing

There are five parts to a golf swing. Nick will demonstrate how each of these parts fits together into a smooth swing.

The Takeaway

In the **takeaway,** Nick moves his club away from the ball. Nick keeps the club in front of his body as he lifts the club. As his arms and shoulders turn, the shaft of the club stays parallel to the target and the ground.

The Backswing

On the **backswing**, Nick cocks his wrists. At the same time, he turns his left forearm. All the while, his shoulders are turning until his back faces the target. Nick also shifts most of his weight to his right leg. This coiling motion will give Nick the power he needs to hit the ball. Nick's legs should resemble a cat's, ready to pounce.

The Downswing

Nick's **downswing** brings the club to the ball on the same path it went up. To do this, Nick shifts his weight from his right leg to his left leg. He moves his hips, legs, and knees as if he were skipping a stone.

As his lower body moves, Nick drops his hands and arms in toward his right side. Nick begins to uncock his wrists. The club goes through the same position that it was in during the takeaway—parallel to the target and the ground.

27

The Swing's the Thing

Here's a practice drill to improve your swing. Place a golf ball 18 inches behind the ball you are going to hit. At the beginning of your stroke, swing the clubhead up and over the back ball. On the downswing, swing the clubhead on a path just inside of the back ball.

The Point of Impact

The club face should be facing the target as it strikes the ball. To make this happen, Nick rotates his left forearm back to its original starting position as he brings down the club.

Also, Nick turns his hips out of the way. This allows his legs, knees, and his right foot to move toward the target, just like the motion of a pitcher throwing to home plate.

The Follow-Through

Nick swings so that his club is parallel to the target and the ground after he has hit the ball. This is his **follow-through**.

When he finishes his follow-through, Nick's shoulders, hips, and knees face the target. His arms are across his chest, and his club is over his left shoulder. Most of his weight is on his left foot and his right foot is up on its toe.

Your golf swing can be as graceful and artistic as a ballerina's pirouette or a gymnast's back flip. Just bring the club back slowly from the ball and gradually increase the speed of your swing. You should be swinging the club as fast as you can when you hit the ball.

Practice your swing at your own pace. Practice placing your body and the club into each of the five positions. With time and practice, you will master the golf swing. Then when you're playing, trust what you've worked on and believe in yourself.

Iron Out a Practice Routine

Hit with the wedge, then the 9-, 8-, and 7-irons when you go out to practice. Once you are warmed up, hit your longer clubs. It's always fun to see how far you can hit the ball. But trying to hit the ball too hard too soon can lead to a poor swing.

Chapter 4

THE WAY TO PLAY

Golfers try to hit a ball into a small opening in the ground, called a cup or **hole**. The grassy area of the course you play on before reaching it is also called a hole. A golf course has 9 or 18 of these holes.

Eighteen holes make up a complete game, known as a **round**. The term round came from the early golf courses built in Scotland. Many were laid out in a circle with the starting and finishing points near each other.

Golfers play each hole in order. There is no set time limit for a golfer to play a hole. Golfers try to use the fewest possible **strokes** to finish a hole.

Getting Better

Do you want to become a better golfer? The professionals at most courses give private lessons. Ask the pro at a course near you if he or she teaches young golfers. Also ask what he or she charges.

Many community education programs and recreation centers offer golf classes or group lessons. Or, borrow golf videos from the library or video store. And don't forget to practice!

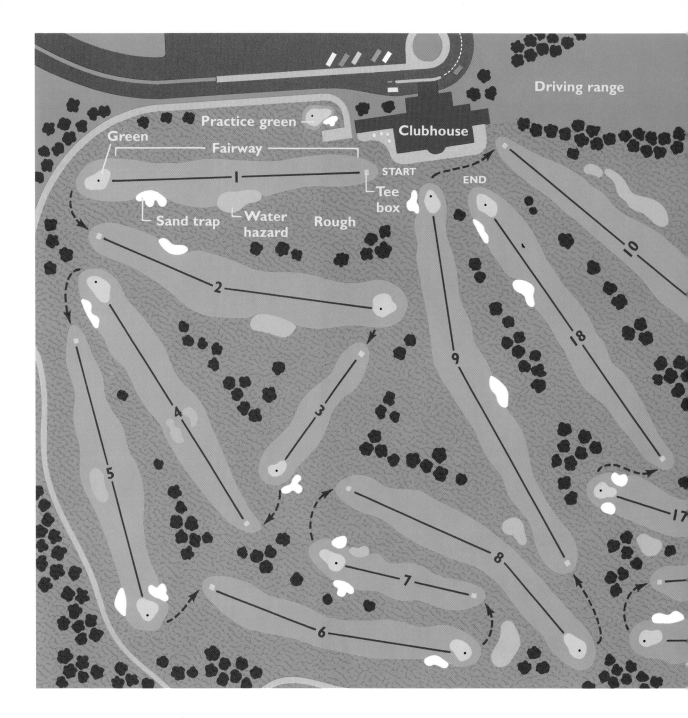

Each hole is made up of a **tee box**, a **fairway**, **rough**, **hazards**, and a **green**. You start to play a hole on the tee box. You hit the ball over the fairway to the green, where you hit it into the cup. You try to avoid the rough and the hazards, which are designed to make playing tougher.

The tee box has two markers. The ball must be hit between the two markers. You may hit your first shot off of a 2-inch wooden peg called a **tee**.

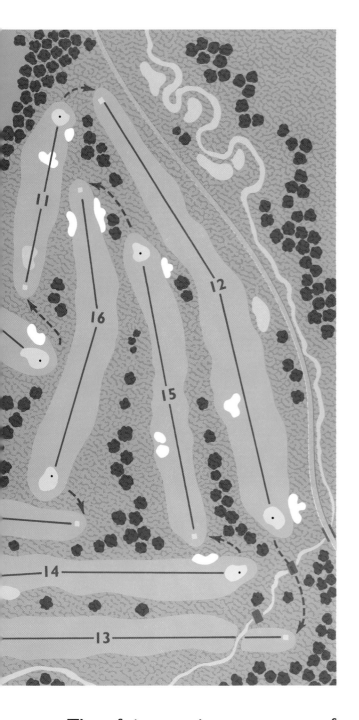

Tournament Time

Golf tournaments can be run two ways—stroke play or match play. Most tournaments use stroke play competition. In a stroke-play tournament, the golfer who took the fewest number of strokes is the winner.

Match play is played by holes. The object of match play is to win more holes than your opponent.

For example, if Jeff makes a 3 on the first hole and Bob scores a 5, Jeff wins the hole. Jeff is one hole up. If, on the second hole, Bob makes a 2 and Jeff makes a 7, Bob wins the hole. The match is even.

A match is played over 18 holes. If Bob and Jeff are tied after 18 holes, the match goes to overtime. Then, the first person to win a hole is the winner.

The fairway is an area of grass between the tee box and the green. The grass is about 1 to 2 inches high. The rough is around the fairway. The grass in the rough is 3 to 6 inches high. Hazards are ponds, streams, and large, shallow holes that are filled with sand.

The grass on the green is cut shorter than the fairway grass. The cup is on the green. The cup is 4¼ inches in diameter and 4 inches deep. There is a 6-foot pole with a flag on top of it in the cup, called a **flagstick**, or **pin**.

Once you have hit your ball into the cup, you are done with that hole. Your score is the number of times you hit the ball.

Golf's Handicap System

*A **handicap** is the average number of strokes a golfer shoots over par. This number is subtracted from the golfer's actual score.*

For instance, John usually shoots a score of 95 for 18 holes. His average score is 23 shots higher than par, so his handicap is 23. If John shot a 93 for 18 holes, he would subtract 23 from his score and his net score would be 70. This means he beat the par-72 course by two shots.

Handicaps range from 0 to 36. Golfers turn in their scorecards to the course pro after playing a round to figure out their handicaps.

Scoring

A skilled golfer is supposed to use a certain number of strokes to play each hole. That number is called **par**. Holes can be 100 to 600 yards long. Holes that are fewer than 250 yards long are expected to be played in three strokes. Holes that are 250 to 475 yards are meant to be played in four strokes. Holes longer than 475 yards are meant to be played in five strokes.

If you use the same number of strokes as par to play a hole, you have shot par, or parred the hole. If you play a hole with one stroke less than par, you have shot a **birdie**. When you take one stroke more than par, you have shot a **bogey**.

Most golf courses have 4 par-3 holes, 4 par-5 holes and 10 par-4 holes. The 18 pars add up to 72. So, the goal is to shoot a score lower than 72.

Of course, when you are learning to play you will have your own goals. Maybe you will want to keep your score on each hole to fewer than 10 strokes. Don't get discouraged if par seems a long way off. Just try to do your best, one shot at a time, and see if you can keep getting better.

Rules

Like other sports, golf has rules. When a player breaks a rule, a shot is added to his or her score as a **penalty stroke.**

For example, Angie has hit her ball into the water. She can't hit it from where it landed, so she must take a penalty of one

shot. Then she can fish her ball out from the water and keep playing.

If her ball is too far in the pond for her to reach, she can use another ball. To do this, Angie drops the new ball within one club length of where her ball went into the water.

Sarah's ball is up against a tree and she can't hit it. She takes a penalty of one shot to move her ball away from the tree. She can't move the ball closer to the cup, however.

When playing golf, the players, not an umpire, decide if a rule has been broken. That's why golf is a great game for developing character!

Etiquette

Golf also has its own special set of manners, or etiquette. These customs make the game fun and fair for everyone. Some of the customs are:

• Be quiet and still while others are making their shots.

• Congratulate a player on a good shot, but don't be critical after a bad one.

• If, after you've hit your ball, you see someone who could get hit by it, yell "Fore!" That warns other golfers that a ball in flight might hit them.

• No more than four people can play a hole at one time.

• While playing a hole, the person whose ball is farthest from the cup hits first. This order of play is followed until the hole is completed by all players.

• Don't rush your shots, but don't dawdle between shots. Always be ready when it is your turn to play.

Marking Your Putt

If your ball is on the green and between another golfer's ball and the cup, you must move it so that the other golfer has a clear path to the cup. To mark your position, slide a coin behind the ball. Then pick up the ball. When you are ready to putt, replace the ball and pick up the coin.

• When playing a round of golf, keep pace with the group in front of yours. If you are falling behind, allow the group behind you to "play through" your group. Let that group tee off on the next hole before your group does.

Chapter 5

SKILL SHOTS

There is more to golf than full swings. Some of the skill shots, such as chipping and pitching, use the full swing as a starting point. But putting demands different skills. These advanced shots take time to learn, but they will help you on the course.

Chips

A short, low shot hit near the green is called a **chip**. You would use a chip shot to hit the ball out of long grass and onto the green. Once on the green, the ball rolls. You want the ball to finish as near to the cup as possible. Use a 7-, 8-, or 9-iron to chip.

To hit a chip shot, Matt grips the club farther down the handle than he would for a full swing. Matt swings his hands, arms, and shoulders together and strikes the ball. There is very little follow-through on a chip, so Matt's club stops soon after it has hit the ball.

Pitch Shots

When there is a sand trap, or **bunker,** between you and the cup, you need to hit the ball so it flies over the bunker and lands on the green. This is called a **pitch** shot.

Gabe is using a 10-iron to hit a pitch shot. His grip is toward the bottom of the handle. He is aiming the clubhead at his target. His body and club are leaning slightly toward the cup.

Gabe moves the club back from the ball and cocks his wrists slightly. As he starts his down-swing, his knees move toward the target. Meanwhile, his wrists uncock toward the ball. When he hits the ball, the loft of the club makes the ball go up. Gabe swings the club for a full follow-through.

Putts

You **putt** on the closely mown area of the golf course called the green. The surface of the green is like the felt covering on a pool table. But a green isn't flat, like a pool table. A green has little slopes and hills. These bumps make the ball roll on curved paths, instead of straight.

The faster the ball rolls, the straighter it rolls. The slower the ball rolls, the more it curves because of the slopes. When putting, you have to decide how hard to hit the ball and what path it will take to the cup.

For example, Matt is putting 20 feet from the hole. The green he is on has a 2-foot slope from right to left. Matt aims the ball 2 feet to the right of the cup and hits it just hard enough to make it go in.

Reading the Green

Before you can putt, you must decide how much a putt will curve. How much slope is there in the green? Which end of the green is higher than the rest? The ball will always curve away from the highest point.

46

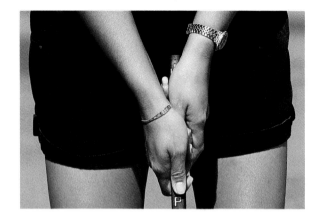

No two golfers putt the same way, just as no two golfers have the same full swing. But every golfer's putting stroke is much simpler than a full swing.

Notice how both of Jenny's thumbs are pointing down at

the clubhead. As she brings the putter away from the ball, Jenny keeps her hands, arms, and shoulders moving together. By doing this, she moves the putter straight back from the ball and then straight to it.

Practice Putts

Put five golf balls in a row on the green. Take a step toward the cup and place a tee in the ground. Keep doing this until you have five tees in the ground. Go back to the row of balls. Try to hit the first ball to the first tee. Then hit the second ball to the next tee. Hit the third ball to the third tee, and so on. This drill will help you learn how hard to hit the ball.

Bunker Shots

When you are hitting your ball out of a bunker, or sand trap, you want to hit the sand 2 inches behind the ball. Then the club can slide underneath the ball. The buildup of sand between the ball and clubhead will blast the ball out of the bunker.

The bottom of a sand wedge is lower than other iron bottoms. This allows the clubhead to slide through the sand. If you don't have a sand wedge, use a 9-iron or pitching wedge.

Reed starts his bunker shot by digging his feet into the sand to keep his balance. Reed uses a full swing, and he swings hard because he will hit sand instead of the ball. Reed follows through so that the sand doesn't slow the clubhead.

If you let your club touch the sand before you begin your swing, you will have to take a penalty stroke. Start your shot with the clubhead at least 1 inch above the sand.

Chapter 6

ON THE COURSE

Learning how to swing the club for various shots will take plenty of practice. But that practice will help you shoot a low score.

Practice also prepares you for playing on the golf course. Out there, you must judge the wind, avoid the sand and water, and deal with the pressure of putting. Let's see how the foursome of Nick, Reed, Sarah, and Jenny put their practice into action.

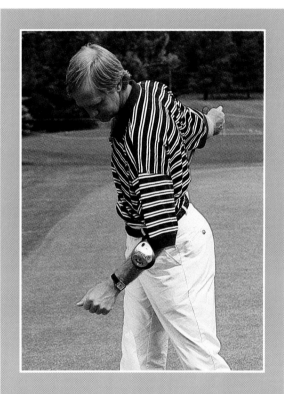

Warming Up

Before you play golf, you need to stretch. Place a club behind your back and between your elbows. Spread your feet shoulder-width apart. Turn to your right and back to your left.

Then place the club behind your back across the shoulder blades and repeat the same twisting motion. In just a few minutes, your muscles are stretched and ready to swing the club.

Hole In One!

*When a golfer hits the ball into the cup with only one stroke, it's a **hole in one**. A hole in one is rare! Most golfers would agree that a golfer has to be lucky to get a hole in one.*

*Holes in one happen most often on par-3 holes. A hole in one on a par-3 is called an **eagle**.*

They are about to play a par-4 hole that is 385 yards long. Golf courses have men's tee boxes and women's tee boxes. Because most women don't hit the ball as far as most men do, the women's tee boxes are closer to the hole. Jenny and Sarah will start playing from the women's tee box.

Nick and Reed will tee off first because their tee box is farther from the hole. Nick swings and hits the ball. It flies down the right side of the fairway. Nick watches as the wind blows the ball to the left. It lands in the middle of the fairway.

Next, Reed places his ball on a brand-new tee. He slowly brings back his club, and whips it down to hit the ball. Reed and Nick watch the ball curve to the right and land in the rough.

Now Sarah takes a couple of practice swings by the women's tee. She swings with a smooth, fluid motion. Her ball lands in the middle of the fairway.

Jenny is the last to tee off. She takes a deep breath, blows it out, and begins her takeaway. Jenny drives the ball forcefully off the tee. But when she looks up, Jenny sees that her ball has landed in the rough to the right. "C'mon Jen," Reed calls. "At least you didn't slice it as bad as I did."

Nick and Sarah walk down the fairway for their second shots. Jenny finds her ball among some small trees. Her ball is about even with Sarah's, but because it curved to the right, it's farther from the hole. Reed, meanwhile, finds his ball even farther to the right than Jenny's, but 20 yards closer to the hole than Nick's ball. Jenny will hit first.

Divot Duty

*Sometimes, when you hit a shot with an iron on the fairway, your clubhead will tear out some turf. This chunk of earth is called a **divot.***

If the divot came from the ground ahead of where your ball was, you're hitting the ball correctly. If the divot came out before you hit the ball, you goofed. Often this happens if you are trying to lift the ball up into the air. Remember, the club's loft will do this.

Always replace the turf that you dug up. Simply place the divot back in the ground and step on it. This gives the grass a chance to grow back.

Jenny decides to use her 7-iron. She wants to hit the ball over the bunker in front of the green. Jenny swings and hits the ball solidly. But the wind blows her ball into the bunker. "Tough luck Jen," Sarah calls. "But you're good in the sand!"

Sarah closes her eyes and pictures the 7-iron shot she wants to hit. Then she takes a deep breath and swings. It's a beautiful shot, heading straight for the pin. The ball lands on the fairway. It's just a couple of yards in front of the green.

Nick chooses to use his 9-iron. His strong, balanced swing produces a solid shot. He looks up to see his ball land softly on the green, 15 feet from the cup.

Reed's ball is in some tall, thick grass in the rough. He will use his 9-iron to power it out of the grass. Reed's swing is a good one, but the wind blows the ball into the bunker. "You don't have to keep me company, Reed," Jenny teases. "Didn't want you to get lonely," says Reed. Nick says, "I'm the one who's lonely, all by myself on the green." Sarah throws a golf towel at him.

Jenny walks into the bunker holding her sand wedge. Jenny's swing slides the clubhead underneath the ball. The force of her swing produces a shower of sand, and the ball comes flying out. Her ball lands on the green and rolls to within 3 feet of the cup. She heaves a big sigh of relief.

Reed walks out and wiggles his feet into the sand. "Keep your fingers crossed," he says to his friends. His shot also comes blasting out of the bunker in a spray of sand, but his ball rolls past the cup and about 20 feet down a slope.

As Reed rakes the sand, Sarah plans her shot. She swings her 9-iron and gently launches the ball. It lands about

Business in a Bunker

Your feet and club will mess up the sand as you hit a bunker shot. After your shot, grab a rake and rake the sand until the surface is smooth again.

20 feet from the cup and rolls down a small slope to within 10 feet of the pin.

Reed putts first. He had been studying the uphill slope of the green while Sarah was chipping. Now he aims for the right of the cup. He hits the ball firmly, but not too hard. The ball climbs up the slope and curves to the left, but rolls to a stop 2 feet short of the cup.

Patching Pitch Marks

When a golf ball lands on the green, it will leave a small dent. These dents are called pitch marks. To repair a mark, stick a tee into the edges of the mark. Gently push the sides into the middle. Then, take your putter and gently tap down on the repaired area. Always repair your own marks and, when possible, other marks.

As Reed putted, Nick was planning his putt. As he crouches behind the ball, Nick sees that the slope of the green is from his left to his right. He

carefully aims the club and gently swings the putter. The ball starts rolling.

Nick gets worried. Did I hit it too hard? Is it going to curve in or not? Then he hears the gentle "plop" of the ball falling into the metal cup. A birdie! He has beaten the hole by using one stroke less than par. "Wow, way to go Nick!" "Nice shot buddy!" Nick grins as his friends congratulate him.

Sarah's ball is about 10 feet from the cup, but it looks like she has a straight-on shot. Sarah bends over the ball, slowly draws back her putter, and taps the ball. She holds her breath as her ball heads straight for the hole, catches the lip of the cup, and bounces away.

Jenny faces a 3-foot putt up the slope. She imagines the ball rolling into the hole as she practices her stroke. When she hits the ball, it rolls right into the center of the cup.

Then Reed steps up for his second putt. This time the ball is about 2 feet from the cup. He taps the ball, gently but firmly. Reed sighs with relief as it falls

decides to aim the ball about 6 inches to the left of the cup.

Nick walks up to the ball and thinks about how hard he should swing the putter. He

into the cup. "OK, Sarah, finish it off," he says and Sarah taps in her ball from 6 inches away.

The four friends walk toward the next hole so that the players behind them can hit onto the green. But before they begin playing again, they stop to figure out their scores. "You're the bogey man, Reed," Nick says. "Oh yeah, well just watch me on this hole. I love these par-5s," Reed says, smiling. "I'm staying out of trouble on this one," Jenny vows. "No rough and no sand for me!"

If you want to test your abilities—like Reed, Nick, Jenny, and Sarah—head for the golf course or the practice range. With blue sky above you and green grass beneath your feet, you'll discover how much fun you can have playing golf.

GOLF TALK

backswing: The motion of the golfer and club that brings the club away from the ball and up.

birdie: A score that is one stroke less than par.

bogey: A score that is one stroke more than par.

bunker: A depression in a fairway or next to a green that is filled with sand.

chip: A short, low shot that is made from close to the green. The golfer intends for the ball to roll across the green after it lands.

course: A series of holes, usually 18 but sometimes 9, that are laid out over a grassy area. The holes are numbered consecutively.

cup: The 4¼-inch hole on a green into which the ball is hit.

divot: A piece of turf that is dug up by a clubhead during a swing.

downswing: The motion of the golfer and club that brings the club down and toward the ball.

eagle: A score that is two shots less than par.

face: The surface of the clubhead that strikes the ball.

fairway: The area between the tee box and the green that is designed to be played on. The grass on the fairway is cut shorter than the rough but not as short as the grass on the green.

follow-through: The motion of the golfer and club that completes a swing after the ball has been hit.

green: A smooth area around the cup where the grass is cut very short.

grip: The way a golfer holds a club. Also, the portion of a club a golfer holds.

handicap: The average number of strokes over par a golfer plays. This number is subtracted from that player's score.

hazard: An obstacle on the course designed to make playing more difficult, such as a bunker or pond.

heel: The portion of the club that joins the shaft to the clubhead.

hole: An area of a course, defined at the start by the tee box and at the finish by the green, over which a golfer hits the ball. Also, the cup on a green.

hole in one: A first stroke on a hole that knocks the ball in the cup.

hook: A shot that curves from right to left, for a right-handed golfer.

iron: A club with a thin metal head and a grooved face that is tilted.

links: Originally a course on sandy strips of land between the ocean and the mainland. Now links is a nickname for any course.

loft: The angle between a club's shaft and clubhead. The greater the angle, the higher the ball will fly.

par: The number of strokes a golfer is expected to use to complete a hole. Par is set for each hole, depending on its length.

penalty stroke: A stroke added to a player's score when that player has broken a rule.

pin: A slender 6-foot pole with a flag at the top. A pin is stuck in each cup to show golfers the cup's location. Also called a **flagstick.**

pitch: A short, high shot, usually hit over water or a bunker. The golfer intends for the ball to stay where it lands on the green and not to roll.

putt: A stroke used when on the green that is designed to roll the ball toward the cup.

putter: A club with a long, flat hitting surface that starts the ball rolling on the green.

rough: The area on a course where grass and weeds aren't mowed. Often there are bushes and trees in the rough also.

round: A complete game of golf (18 holes).

set-up: The position a golfer assumes before hitting the ball.

slice: A shot that curves from left to right, for a right-handed golfer.

stroke: The motion a golfer uses to hit the ball. Also called a **swing.**

takeaway: The early part of the backswing during which the club is pulled back away from the ball.

tee: A small wooden or plastic peg on which the ball is placed before the first shot of a hole.

tee box: The marked area at the start of a hole from which a golfer's first shot is hit.

toe: The part of the clubhead farthest from the shaft.

wood: A club with a large clubhead and a flat hitting surface.

FURTHER READING

Lopez, Nancy. *Nancy Lopez's The Complete Golfer.* Chicago, Illinois: Contemporary Books, Inc., 1987.

McCormick, Bill. *The Complete Beginner's Guide to Golf.* New York: Doubleday & Company, Inc., 1974.

Mulvoy, Mark. *Sports Illustrated Golf.* New York: Harper & Row, Publishers, 1983.

Wiren, Gary. *The PGA Manual of Golf.* New York: Macmillan Publishing Company, 1991.

FOR MORE INFORMATION

American Junior Golf Association
2415 Steeplechase Lane
Roswell, GA 30076

Hook A Kid On Golf
2611 Old Okeechobee Road
West Palm Beach, FL 33409

Ladies' Professional Golf Association
2570 Volusia Avenue, Suite B
Daytona Beach, FL 32114

Professional Golfers Association of
   America
100 Avenue of the Champions
PO Box 109601
Palm Beach Gardens, FL 33410

United States Golf Association
Liberty Corner Road
Far Hills, NJ 07931

INDEX